530.8 Measurem

PATCHAM HIGH SCHOOL
LADIES MILE ROAD
BRIGHTON
EAST SUSSEX BN1 8PB

be returned on or before
st date below.

MEASURING

Contributory Author
Brian Knapp, BSc, PhD
Art Director
Duncan McCrae, BSc
Special models
*Tim Fulford, MA, Head of Design and Technology,
Leighton Park School*
Special photography
Graham Servante
Editorial consultant
Rita Owen
Illustrations
David Woodroffe
Science advisor
*Jack Brettle, BSc, PhD, Chief Research Scientist,
Pilkington plc*
Print consultants
Landmark Production Consultants Ltd
Printed and bound in Hong Kong
Produced by
EARTHSCAPE EDITIONS

First published in the United Kingdom in 1992
by Atlantic Europe Publishing Company Limited,
86 Peppard Road, Sonning Common, Reading,
Berkshire, RG4 9RP, UK

Copyright © 1992
Atlantic Europe Publishing Company Limited

Publication Data

Knapp, Brian
  Measuring – (Science in our world; 18)
  1. Mensuration – For children
  I. Title   II. Series
530.8

ISBN 1-869860-66-7

All rights reserved. No part of this publication may be reproduced, stored in a retrieval system, or transmitted in any form or by any means otherwise, without prior permission in writing of the publisher, nor be otherwise circulated in any form of binding or cover other than that in which it is published and without a similar condition including this condition being imposed on the subsequent purchaser.

In this book you will find some words that have been shown in **bold** type. There is a full explanation of each of these words on pages 46 and 47.

On many pages you will find experiments that you might like to try for yourself. They have been put in a yellow box like this.

In this book
m stands for metres,
cm stands for centimetres,
km stands for kilometres,
l stands for litres,
ml stands for millilitres and
g stands for grams.

Acknowledgements
The publishers would like to thank the following:
Leighton Park School, Micklands County Primary School, Redlands County Primary School, Margaret and John Pink and Dr Andrew Burnett.

Picture credits
t=top b=bottom l=left r=right

All photographs from the Earthscape Editions photographic library except the following:
David Higgs 14, Tim Fulford 28, ZEFA 22/23.

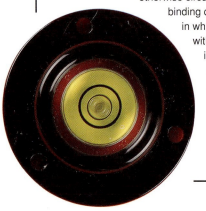

Contents

Introduction	Page	4
Short lengths		6
Difficult distances		8
Areas		10
Volume		12
Irregular shapes		14
Circles and spheres		16
Weight		18
Sensitive measurement		20
Speed and acceleration		22
Air pressure		24
Liquid pressure		26
Flow		28
Upright and level		30
Temperature		32
Light and colour		34
Electricity		36
Using a meter		38
Acidity		40
Pollution		42
Samples		44
New words		46
Index		48

Introduction

rulers page 6

weight page 20

pollution page 42

circles page 18

odd shapes page 16

air pressure page 24

Look at the hands of a watch measuring the time; run your finger over the marks on a ruler, measuring length. There are often times in our daily lives when accurate measurements of the things we use are important. For example, when we need to find out how much medicine we must take to make us better or how much of each ingredient to put into a cake.

Measuring, however, is not simply counting. It is *using* counting to find out about the world. But if we are going to measure something we have to have a basic 'ruler' to measure it with. For example, the 'ruler' for time is the second and the 'ruler' for electricity is called the amp.

Every kind of measurement needs a 'ruler' and so people have to agree what the

samples page 44

speed page 22

areas page 12

meter page 38

4

blood pressure
page 26

fluid flow
page 28

sensitivity
page 10

level
page 30

acidity
page 40

volume
page 14

divisions on the 'ruler' should be. In the past people in different countries developed their own kinds of measurement based on practical distances they needed for their everyday lives. But having many different kinds of measurement is awkward, because it means that measurements cannot easily be compared between countries.

Today there are two main systems for measuring: the **metric** system (which uses metres for length, kilograms for weight and litres for volume), and the **imperial** system, which uses the foot for length, the pound for weight and the quart for volume.

In this book you can find out about some of the many methods that have been developed to measure our world. Just turn to a page to begin your discoveries.

electricity
page 36

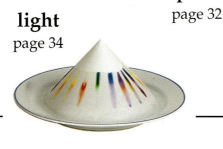

light
page 34

temperature
page 32

callipers
page 8

5

Short lengths

Length is one of the most common measurements that people make. If you want to know the size of a piece of paper, the length of carpet needed to fit a room, or the distance from one city to another, you will need to use some form of ruler or rule.

There are many kinds of ruler, each suited to the distances and accuracies that are needed. On this page you will find some common ways of measuring short distances.

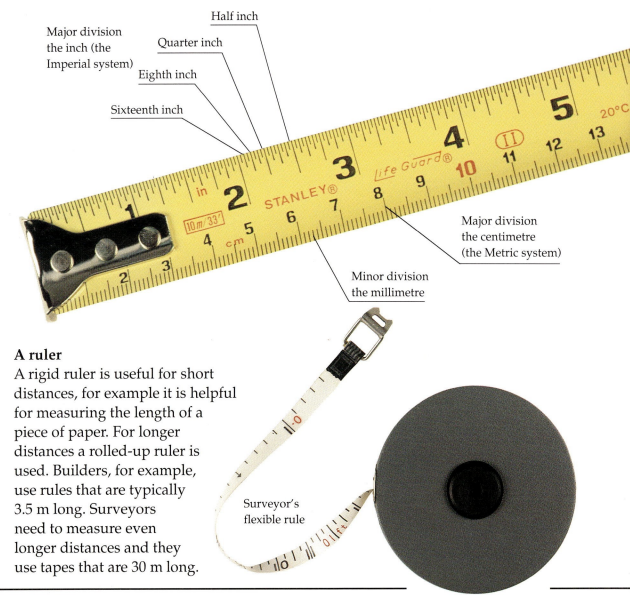

A ruler
A rigid ruler is useful for short distances, for example it is helpful for measuring the length of a piece of paper. For longer distances a rolled-up ruler is used. Builders, for example, use rules that are typically 3.5 m long. Surveyors need to measure even longer distances and they use tapes that are 30 m long.

A builder's flexible rule

Sound rulers
Rulers do not have to be lengths of metal, wood or plastic. Distances of a few metres can be measured quite accurately by using a sound beam.

Sound travels at a known speed and the instrument on the right is designed to measure how long it takes for a sound signal to be bounced back from its destination.

Difficult distances

Many lengths cannot easily be measured with an ordinary ruler. Think of trying to measure the distance from one city to another using an ordinary ruler, or measuring the size of an egg. In order to measure these lengths other kinds of measuring instruments are needed. Some of them are shown here.

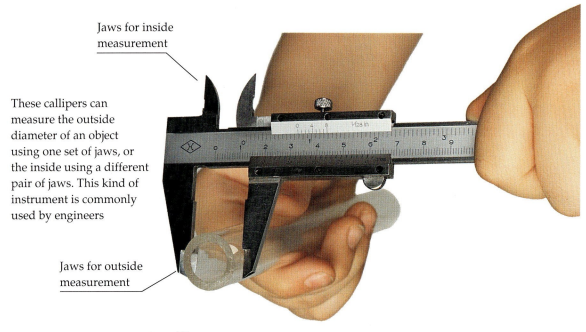

Jaws for inside measurement

These callipers can measure the outside diameter of an object using one set of jaws, or the inside using a different pair of jaws. This kind of instrument is commonly used by engineers

Jaws for outside measurement

A calliper
The width of solid objects is often difficult to measure with a ruler. Callipers are used instead. These are like pincers, used as shown in the pictures on these pages. The width is measured off the calliper scale.

Measuring road distances

When planning journeys it is useful to know the distance, because you can use this information to work out how long it will take to get to your destination.

Road distances are usually measured with a **calibrated** wheel. This is called an odometer. Cars have odometers on their dashboards, often with a facility for resetting so that you can see how far you have travelled on a particular journey.

A vernier

This is a special extra scale, used for additional accuracy. The vernier scale is divided into a hundred equal parts, with one full rotation of the vernier moving on one division of the horizontal scale. The horizontal scale in the picture reads just over 20 mm, the vernier shows that the more accurate reading is 20.28 mm.

This special scale (called a vernier) is used when very accurate measurements are needed. This scale can measure to one hundredth of a millimetre!

Measure road distances

You can measure road distances using a bicycle wheel as an odometer.

Make a clear chalk mark where the front tyre rests on the ground, then push the wheel a complete **revolution**. Use a ruler to measure this distance (called the circumference, see page 17).

Place the tyre with the chalk mark down over the place you want to measure from, then push the bike, keeping count of the number of complete revolutions made before you get to your destination.

You then multiply the number of revolutions by the circumference and you will have the answer to how far you have travelled.

Areas

The amount of surface something has is called its area.

There are many kinds of area that need to be measured, and there are several ways of doing it. One of the easiest is by counting squares.

Measuring squares

A square is a shape where there are four corners at right angles to each other and where each side has the same length. The chess board in the picture below is made of square pieces of decorative stone. Each square has a side measuring 4 cm.

The area of a square is found by multiplying the length of two of its sides. So

> 4 cm x 4 cm = 16 cm squared.

Many squares
How many different sized square shapes can you find on this chess board?

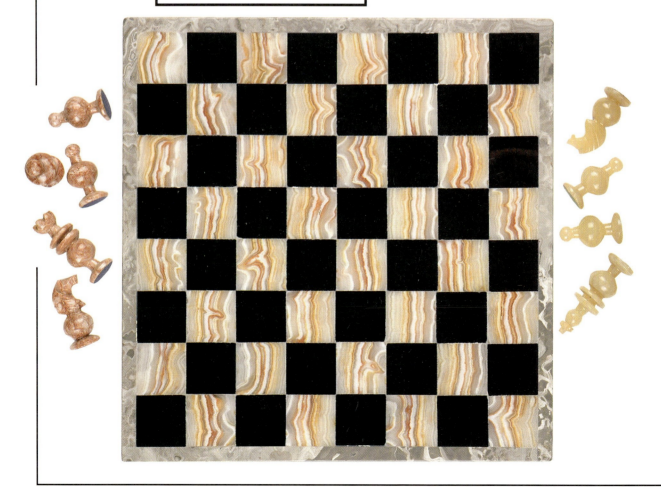

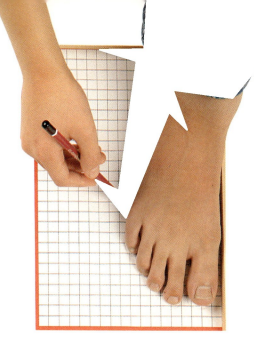

Using squared paper
You can get specially printed paper called graph paper, marked with squares. The squares usually have sides 1 cm long with divisions of 1 mm.

Try to find the area of a small object by placing it on squared paper and drawing round its base.

Count the squares the object covers and you know what area it has.

Areas
Using the chess board you can find out the areas of many differently-sized squares. The whole playing surface of the chess board has sides eight squares long. The whole board therefore consists of 64 squares. Can you calculate the area of the playing surface in square centimetres?

Measuring the area of an irregular shape
Some shapes do not have straight sides. The profiles of people, for example, have a very irregular shape.

To find the area of people you could use a piece of plastic netting drawn tightly over their profiles. The area of a profile is now found by counting how many squares it covers.

Why would you need a different size of mesh if you are making more precise measurements?

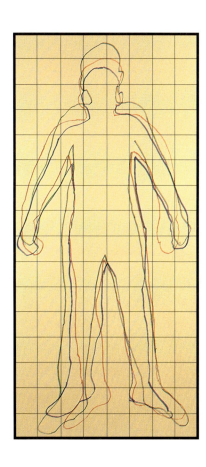

Rectangles
The left hand half of the chess board is said to be the 'home' area of the red player. This shape is only four squares by eight. This area does not have sides of equal length, and it is called a **rectangle**.

The area of a rectangle is found by multiplying one of the longer sides (8) by one of the shorter ones (4). What is the 'home' area of the red player in square centimetres?

Volume

(For more information on cubes and other solid shapes see the book Patterns and Shapes *in the Science in our world series.)*

How much space something occupies is known as its volume.

Although some shapes are easy to measure, others need a bit of imagination if you are to find out their volumes without ruining them.

Volumes of simple shapes
Just as it was easy to work out the area of a simple shape, so it is easy to work out its volume. This box has all equal sides; it is called a cube.

You can work out the volume of a cube by multiplying together the lengths of any three sides. In this case because they are all 15 cm long, the volume is

$$15 \times 15 \times 15 = 3375 \text{ ml}$$

A cube

Measure volumes
Volumes are used to measure many ingredients in cooking just as they are used to measure ingredients for making cement or for measuring volumes of medicines. In each case it is important to have a simple way of measuring the volumes used.

You can make a volume measurer for dry material such as sugar with a sheet of card and a strip of transparent adhesive tape.

The size of the container is a matter of choice. The one shown on the opposite page has a **capacity** of 250 ml. The area of the base of the container is 25 cm squared. The volume is found by multiplying the area of the base by the height. A container 10 cm high will hold 5 x 5 x 10 = 250 ml .

Cut out the shape shown opposite and mark the card next to the slot into 1 cm lengths, starting from the base. Thus the tube filled to the 1 cm mark will hold 25 ml and so on.

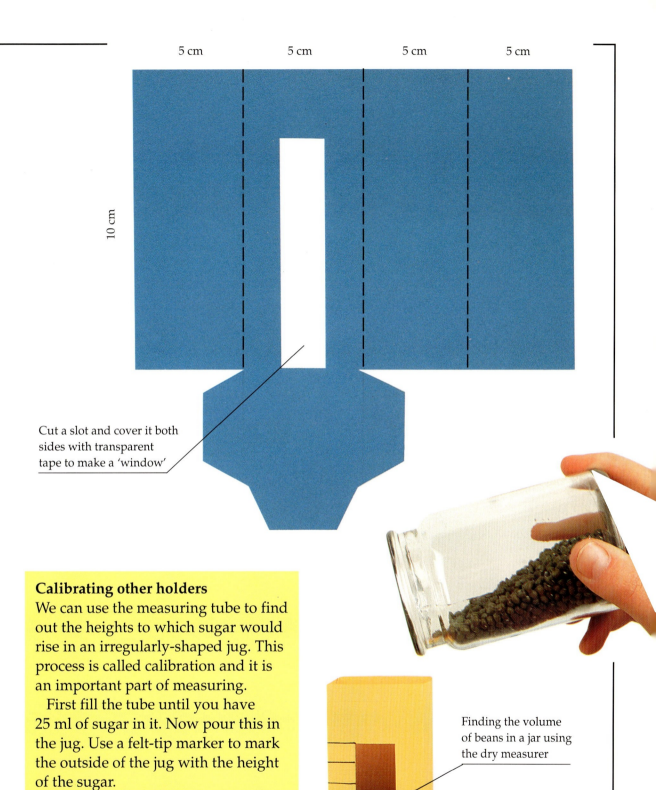

5 cm   5 cm   5 cm   5 cm

10 cm

Cut a slot and cover it both sides with transparent tape to make a 'window'

Calibrating other holders

We can use the measuring tube to find out the heights to which sugar would rise in an irregularly-shaped jug. This process is called calibration and it is an important part of measuring.

First fill the tube until you have 25 ml of sugar in it. Now pour this in the jug. Use a felt-tip marker to mark the outside of the jug with the height of the sugar.

Repeat this step, 25 ml at a time, marking the jug as you go. If you now pour the sugar out you can use the jug to measure the volumes of liquids such as milk.

Finding the volume of beans in a jar using the dry measurer

Irregular shapes

Irregularly-shaped objects are among the most difficult things to measure. For example, how do you measure the size of a doll or a turtle?

Here are some suggestions.

Growing healthy
Scientists want to measure how fast healthy turtles grow in order that they will know how to care for the sick or injured. But what would be the best measure of growth – length, weight, or volume? Volume might be the best measure, but it can also be the most awkward, particularly when dealing with an active animal.

Moving objects
One possible way to measure the volume of a turtle is by placing it in a container and filling it to the brim with water. Remove the turtle and see how much more water must be added to fill the container again. Can you suggest some practical problems that might have to be overcome?

Measuring by differences
Take a jug and stand it in a tray. Place a doll or any other object whose volume you want to measure in the jug and then add salt until the salt completely covers the object. Note the volume as marked on the side of the jug.

Carefully pour the salt into another jug and find its volume. The difference between the two measurements will be the volume of the object.

Think of some ways you can make these measurements more accurate. Do you have a more accurately marked scientific **measuring cylinder** for example?

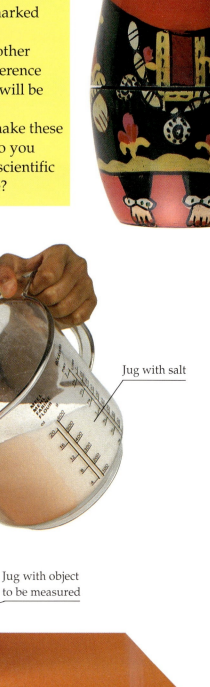

Jug with salt

Jug with object to be measured

15

Circles and spheres

To work out the sizes of circles and spheres you have to follow a special set of rules, which will let you measure or calculate everything from the size of your bicycle wheel to the volume of the Earth.

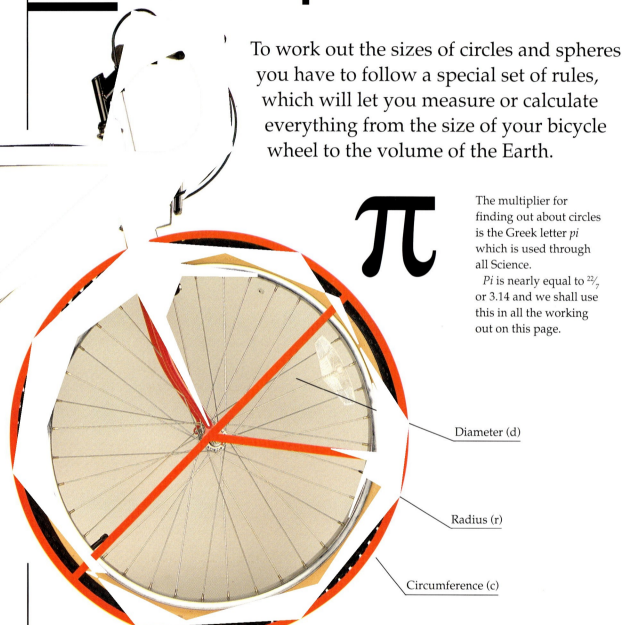

π

The multiplier for finding out about circles is the Greek letter *pi* which is used through all Science.

Pi is nearly equal to $\frac{22}{7}$ or 3.14 and we shall use this in all the working out on this page.

Diameter (d)

Radius (r)

Circumference (c)

The equations are:

Circumference $= 2 \times \pi \times r$
$\qquad\qquad\quad\; = 2 \times \frac{22}{7} \times r$

Area $= \pi \times r \times r = \frac{22}{7} \times r \times r$

Volume of sphere $= \frac{4}{3} \times \pi \times r \times r \times r$
$\qquad\qquad\qquad\; = \frac{4}{3} \times \frac{22}{7} \times r \times r \times r$

Measuring the properties of a bicycle wheel
A wheel is a circle. Thousands of years ago Archimedes, a Greek scientist, found out that, no matter how big the circle, there is always the same proportion ($\frac{22}{7}$) between the length measured across it, the area inside the circle and the length round the edge.

Measuring circumference
To measure the radius of a wheel use a ruler held in the centre of the hub and measure to the outside of the tyre. For the circumference, make a mark on the tyre with chalk, then place the mark on the floor and make a chalk mark here too. Now roll the wheel one complete revolution and make a mark on the floor. Use a rule to find the distance for this one revolution. Now work out the circumference using the radius you measured and the appropriate rule on the opposite page. Check to see the measurements and calculations are the same.

Measure the volume of a ball
First find the diameter by holding the ball between two books and measuring the distance between them. Divide this by 2 to find the radius.

Measure the volume of the ball by pushing it into water using the method given on page 14.

Calculate the volume using the appropriate equation opposite. Check to see if the measurement and calculation are the same.

The size of the Earth
The volume of the Earth or its circumference cannot be measured directly, it has to be calculated. The radius of the Earth is known to be 6,700 km. Can you find out how far you would have to travel round the world, using the equations opposite? Can you find the volume of the Earth?

Weight

The heaviness of an object is called its weight. In the metric system the basic unit is the kilogram (kg), whereas in the Imperial system it is the pound (lb).

Goods are commonly sold by weight and a variety of scales have been produced for this purpose. There are several ways of measuring weight, some of which are shown here.

This balance is designed to measure the weight of people. As you stand on the scale pan a strip of springy metal bends slightly, and a pointer attached to the spring moves across a scale

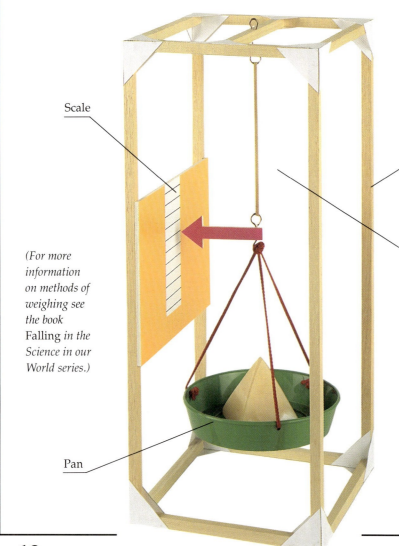

Scale

Wooden frame

Elastic band

Pan

(For more information on methods of weighing see the book Falling *in the* Science in our World *series.)*

Spring balances
These measure how far an elastic material changes length when an object is placed on or hung from it. Many spring balances, such as in the bathroom scales above, use metal. The one shown on the left uses an elastic band. You may like to build it for yourself.

18

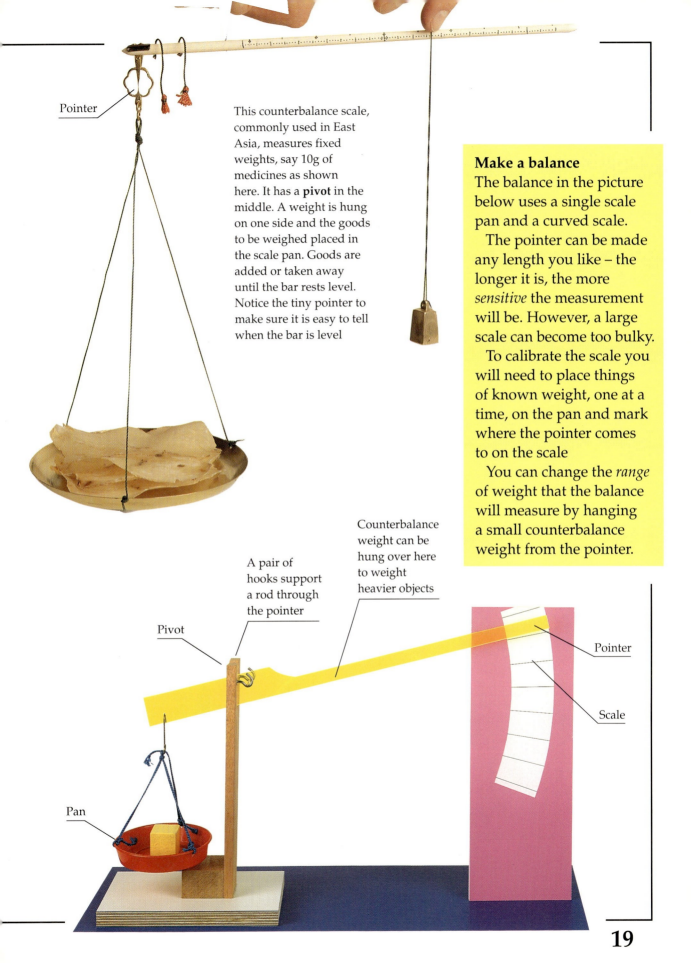

Pointer

This counterbalance scale, commonly used in East Asia, measures fixed weights, say 10g of medicines as shown here. It has a **pivot** in the middle. A weight is hung on one side and the goods to be weighed placed in the scale pan. Goods are added or taken away until the bar rests level. Notice the tiny pointer to make sure it is easy to tell when the bar is level

Make a balance
The balance in the picture below uses a single scale pan and a curved scale.

The pointer can be made any length you like – the longer it is, the more *sensitive* the measurement will be. However, a large scale can become too bulky.

To calibrate the scale you will need to place things of known weight, one at a time, on the pan and mark where the pointer comes to on the scale

You can change the *range* of weight that the balance will measure by hanging a small counterbalance weight from the pointer.

A pair of hooks support a rod through the pointer

Counterbalance weight can be hung over here to weight heavier objects

Pivot

Pointer

Scale

Pan

19

Sensitive measurement

Many small changes are not easy to measure because of the natural stickiness (**friction**) of the joints in the measuring equipment.

But you can easily measure small changes using a beam of light. Here are some suggestions to experiment with.

Enlarging the scale
By using a long beam of light you are making an enlargement of the way the wire moves, just as you use a projector for enlarging pictures (Gently tap a projector to see how it makes the picture shake).

Because a beam of light has no sticky joints it is very sensitive.

Measuring vibration
Here are some suggestions on how to use a vibration meter. Test your vibration meter by striking a tuning fork and placing it on the table near the vibratometer.

Try placing a small loudspeaker next to the mirror end of the blade and then turning the volume up and down.

Place the vibratometer on the floor of a corridor and try to detect feet moving on the floor before you see people coming.

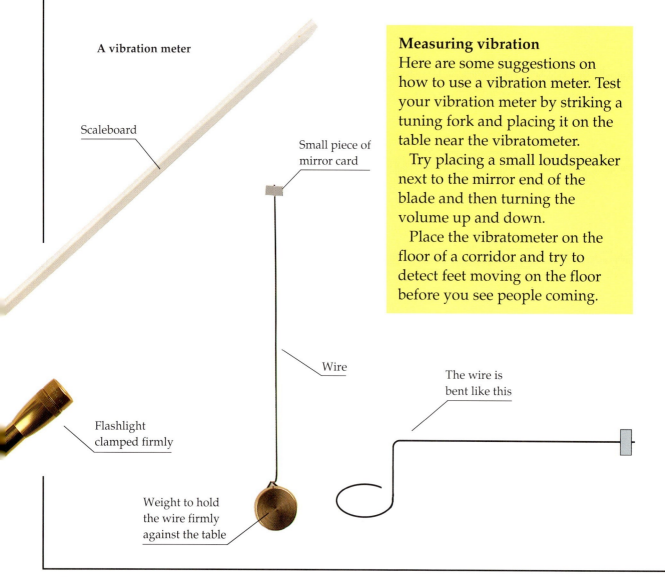

A vibration meter
- Scaleboard
- Small piece of mirror card
- Wire
- The wire is bent like this
- Flashlight clamped firmly
- Weight to hold the wire firmly against the table

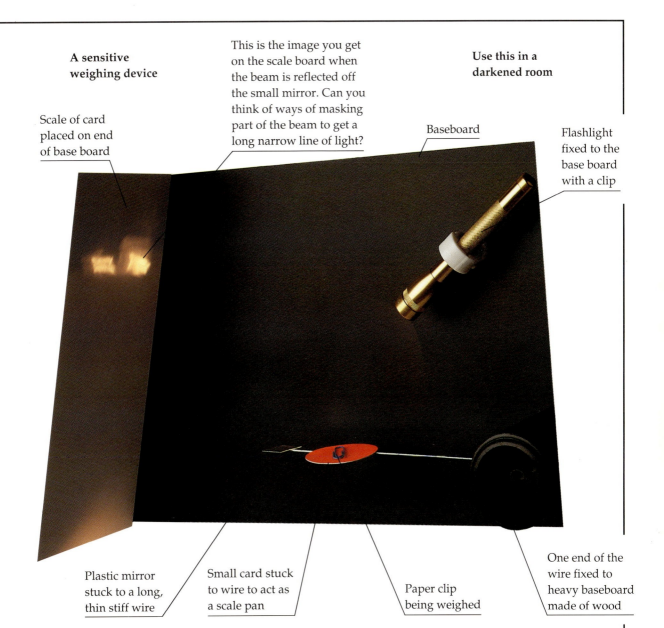

Making a sensitive meter

The springy wire meter is a long thin wire (such as the wire used by florists).

One end of the wire is also fixed to the board and a tiny piece of mirror card is stuck to the free end. You need a source of light such as a flashlight that is firmly fixed to a board by a clip. By using the flashlight beam bounced off the mirror you will easily see any movement that occurs at the end of the wire.

The distance between the flashlight, the wire and the scale will decide how sensitive your meter is. Experiment with distances and the shape of the beam until you are happy with the result. You may also want to enclose part of the equipment so you can see the scale clearly, even in daylight. Fix a scale disc to the wire if you want to use it to measure small changes in weight.

21

Speed and acceleration

Speed is a measure of how fast something is moving. (Velocity, describes how fast something is travelling and the direction in which it is travelling). To measure speed, you have to know the time taken to travel a known distance.

Acceleration is a measure of the rate at which speed changes.

Measure the acceleration of a runner
The runner in the picture below has been taken with a special 'freeze-frame' camera that takes pictures at even intervals.
To find the acceleration of this runner, measure the horizontal distances between each position of his head and then make a chart of distance covered against time.

Average walking speed
For this you need a stop watch and a known distance. Using an athletic track is helpful because the circuit length is known, and the surface is flat and easy to walk on.

The speed of walking is worked out by the distance walked (d) divided by the time it took (t) or

$$\text{speed} = d/t$$

Speed is measured in metres per second or kilometres per hour in the metric system and miles per hour in the Imperial system.

It is difficult to walk at a constant speed. A more accurate result is obtained by walking for longer. This gives you an evened-out or *average* result.

(For other information on starting, see the book Starting and stopping *in the Science in our world series.)*

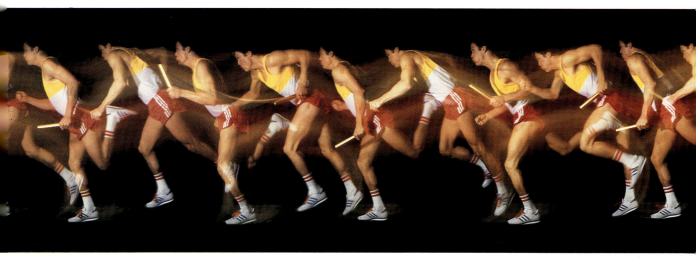

Acceleration

At the start of a race, speed increases. This is called acceleration. Sometimes, when going round a curve, the speed slows down, this is called deceleration.

Acceleration is the *change* in speed. Sometimes it is measured as the time to reach a certain speed from rest (you will find it described this way in motorbike and automobile magazines).

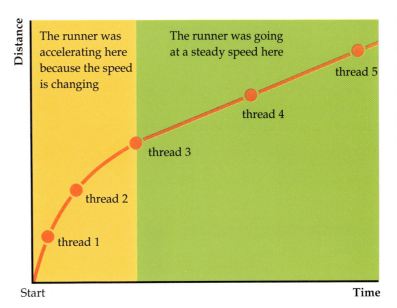

Which kind of race best suits you?
You can try to find your change in speed when you are on a sports field. You need several people each with stop watches spaced at even distances.

Every 20 metres place a thread of cotton across the track at chest height. When the starter shouts 'GO!', all the recorders start their stop watches. Then, as each thread is broken by the runner, the recorders stop their watches. At the end all the times are drawn onto a chart like the one above.

Compare a number of runners to see who makes the fastest get-away to reach the first thread. Should they be the people who take part in short races? Should those with the highest steady speed (between threads 3 and 5) take part in longer distance races? Discuss whether there are other factors involved.

Air pressure

Any **fluid**, such as air or water, can move easily. In the **atmosphere**, the air flows in huge swirling motions from the equator to the poles. As a result the air tends to build up in some places and flow away from others.

Meteorologists call a place where air builds a high pressure region, or anticyclone; a region from which air flows away is called a low pressure region or cyclone.

The most common measurements of air pressure are made with a barometer. This instrument is easy to make and it will help you to forecast the weather.

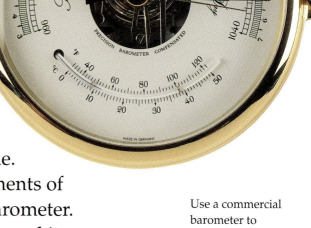

Use a commercial barometer to calibrate the scale of your instrument

> **Make a barometer**
> You can easily make a barometer by cutting a balloon in half and stretching it over the opened end of a jar.
>
> As the pressure decreases in the atmosphere (a low pressure is developing) the volume of the air in the jar will increase (causing the balloon surface to move up). If atmospheric pressure increases (a high pressure is developing) the balloon surface will move down. The pointer is designed to amplify these changes in the height of the balloon surface.
>
> Make a pointer on a pivot (see page 19 for more details) and if necessary add a small piece of modelling clay to the short side of the pointer to keep it gently pressing down on the balloon.
>
> Use a commercial barometer to calibrate your scale and keep the barometer in a room where the temperature remains even.

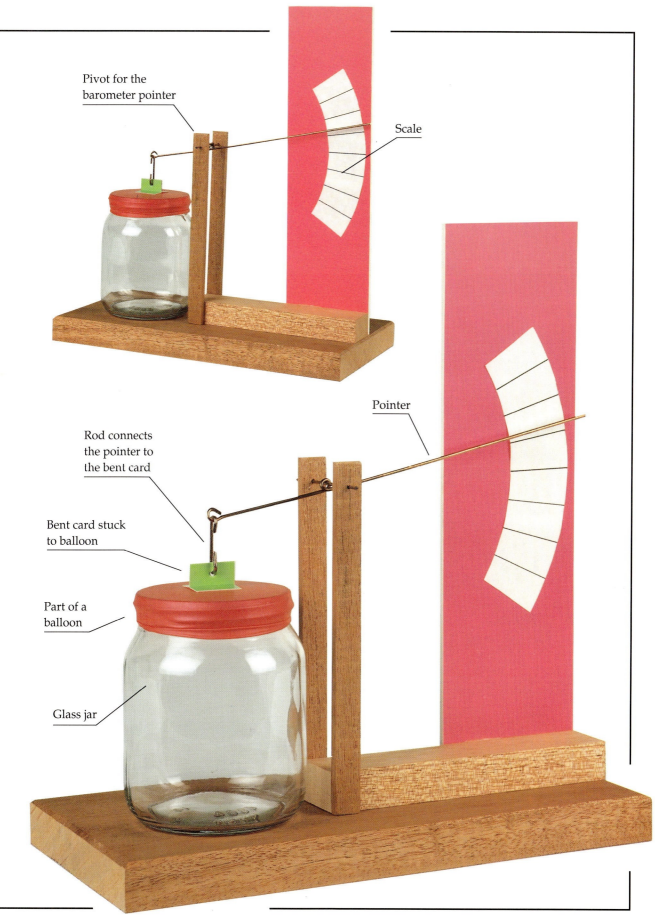

Liquid pressure

The pressure in a tube caused by liquid flowing through it is measured with an instrument called a manometer. This is really a long pipe filled with a liquid. As the fluid flows faster it increases the pressure inside the tube and the level of liquid in the manometer rises against a scale.

A manometer will measure the pressure of water flowing from your tap. It will also measure the way your heart pumps blood around your body.

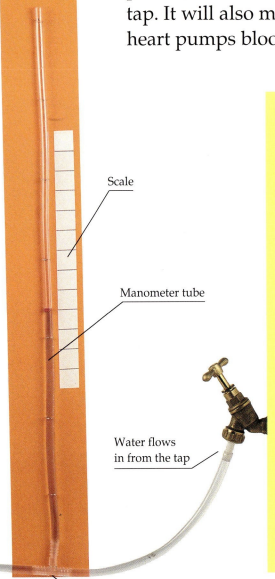

Scale

Manometer tube

Water flows in from the tap

Water is led to the sink

Connecting piece

Make a manometer
You can make a manometer to measure the pressure of water in a tube using a coupling to a tap and some lengths of transparent tubing.

The tubes need to be connected using a 'T' or 'Y'- shaped connecting piece. One tube then goes to the tap, one piece is led into a sink and the final piece is held upright. The upright tube makes the manometer.

When the tap is turned on water flows down the tube and most escapes into the sink. However, as you turn the tap further, and increase the pressure, the water will also start to rise in the upright tube. The height of the water in the manometer tube is a measure of the pressure.

The stethoscope is used to listen for the flow of blood

A qualified medical person must be present when using blood pressure apparatus

This bandage contains an 'inner tube' that is blown up by squeezing the black bulb

The manometer is a tube filled with liquid mercury. It has a scale which allows the blood pressure to be read

Blood pressure

Blood is pumped around our bodies by the heart. Doctors measure the efficiency of a heart by measuring the pressure of blood as it circulates through the **arteries**.

To measure blood pressure, a band, or cuff, containing a rubber 'inner tube' called a bladder is wrapped around the arm and air is pumped into the bladder by squeezing a bulb. Doctors know from experience the pressure needed to stop the blood from flowing.

The doctor now lets out some of the air from the bladder and at the same time listens through a **stethoscope** placed on the arm for when the blood starts to be pumped through the artery again. It makes a faint swishing sound. This pressure can be read on a scale on the manometer (the value might be 150 mm of mercury). Air is then slowly released from the bladder again until all swishing sounds have stopped and the blood flows normally. This pressure (which might be 90 mm of mercury) is also read from the manometer scale.

The two pressures (in our example 150/90) are an important indication of the health of a person.

Flow

It is extremely difficult to see how a colourless substance such as a liquid or a gas, is flowing. As a result, detectors and tracers are used to follow the way these substances move.

(For more information on measuring elements of the weather see the book Weather *in the Science in our World series.)*

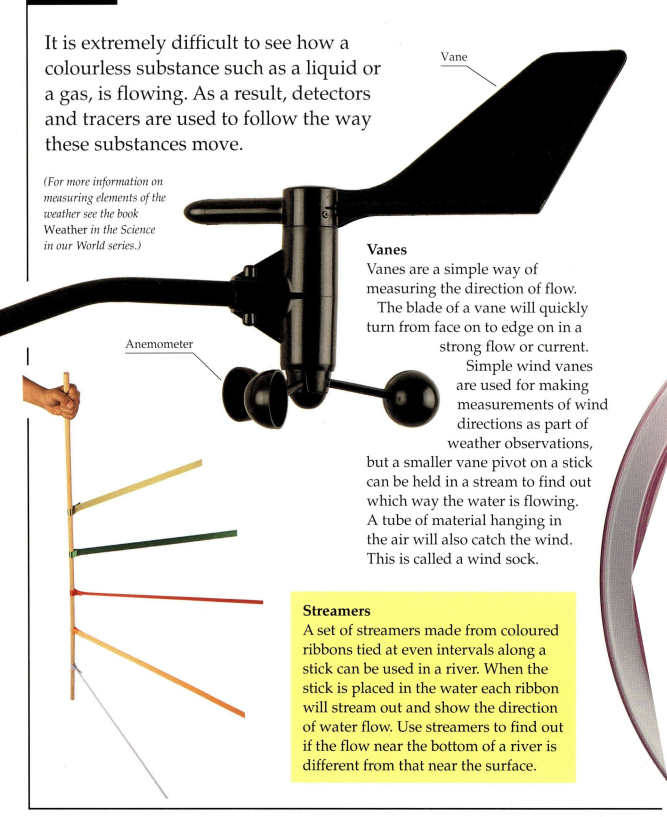

Vanes

Vanes are a simple way of measuring the direction of flow.

The blade of a vane will quickly turn from face on to edge on in a strong flow or current.

Simple wind vanes are used for making measurements of wind directions as part of weather observations, but a smaller vane pivot on a stick can be held in a stream to find out which way the water is flowing. A tube of material hanging in the air will also catch the wind. This is called a wind sock.

Streamers

A set of streamers made from coloured ribbons tied at even intervals along a stick can be used in a river. When the stick is placed in the water each ribbon will stream out and show the direction of water flow. Use streamers to find out if the flow near the bottom of a river is different from that near the surface.

Spinners

One way of measuring wind speed is to use an instrument called an anemometer. This consists of three cups attached to a spindle, as you can see in the picture on the opposite page.

A smaller version of an anemometer placed upside down in a river will measure water speed.

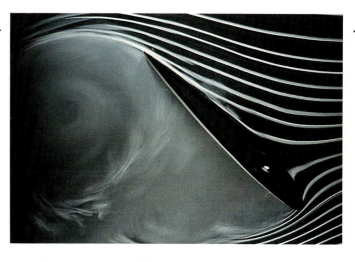

Tracing patterns of flow

One way to find out how a fluid is moving is to trace it using a substance that will mix readily with the fluid.

Gases are often traced using smoke. In the picture above the smoke makes white lines over the section of an aircraft wing. This helps designers to find out how efficient and safe an aircraft design is.

Trace water flow

Place a few crystals of permanganate of potash dropped in a bowl of stirred water to act as a tracer. Watch the changes in pattern as the water slows down

Permanganate of potash crystals tracing swirling water in a dish

Do not put tracing chemicals in a stream or other water supply.

29

Upright and level

There are many occasions when it is important to know that something is level (or horizontal) and upright (or vertical).

Both horizontal and vertical can be found using the properties of **gravity**.

A plumb line
Gravity causes all objects to fall towards the centre of the Earth. If a weight is fastened to cotton thread, it will pull the thread straight and this will make a vertical line, or plumb line.

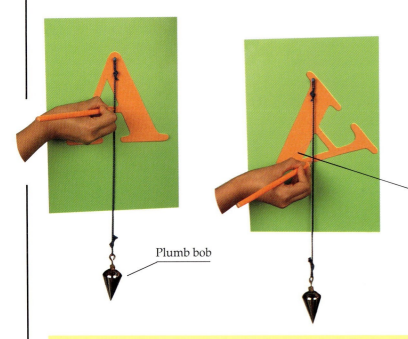

Plumb bob

Pencil line from first use of plumb line

A hanging weight always makes a vertical plumb line

Centre of gravity
Sometimes we want to know where the effective weight of an object lies. This is called the centre of gravity. Objects with a low centre of gravity are not easily knocked over.

The centre of gravity for a cardboard letter, for example, can be found using a plumb line. Suspend the letter so that it can swing freely, for example, by piercing it with a drawing pin. Make a loop in the plumb line thread and hang it over the pin. When the plumb line and the letter come to rest carefully mark the line of the thread on the card using a pencil.

Chose any other place on the letter and use the plumb line in the same way as before. The centre of gravity is located where the pencil lines cross. If you have the centre of gravity correctly marked the letter will balance on, for example, the end of a straw.

A circular spirit level checks the level in all directions

Bubble

Spirit level

A bubble sealed in a liquid-filled banana-shaped tube is called a **spirit** level. It is commonly used to find when something is horizontal or vertical.

An air bubble will always rise to the top of the tube. If the tube is level the bubble will be exactly in the centre of the tube. If the tube is even slightly tilted the bubble will move to the upper end.

Finding levels

Water in a tube will continue to flow until the water levels at each end of the tube are at the same height as each other, no matter how coiled the tube might be. A transparent tube filled with water can therefore be used to find two places that are at the same height even thought they may be out of sight of each other.

Bubble

These two pictures show a spirit level. The body of the level contains two spirit level tubes. One is used to measure when the body of the level is horizontal, the other, when it is vertical. Sprit levels like this are used throughout the building industry

Bubble

Temperature

Temperature is a measure of how hot or cold something is. The most common kind of thermometer uses a thin tube containing a coloured liquid. The liquid is kept in a bulbed reservoir and as the temperature surrounding the thermometer rises, the liquid in the tube expands and pushes the liquid up the tube.

A scale marked on the thermometer gives accurate readings of temperature. Temperature can also be measured electrically, and by using the properties of special chemicals.

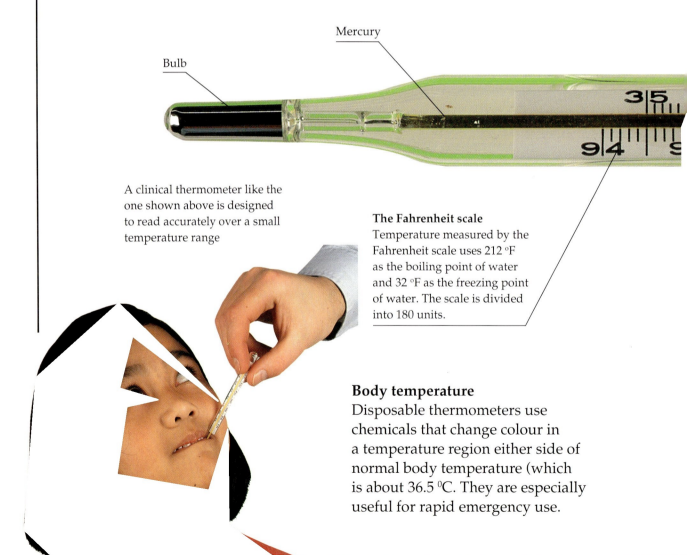

Bulb

Mercury

A clinical thermometer like the one shown above is designed to read accurately over a small temperature range

The Fahrenheit scale
Temperature measured by the Fahrenheit scale uses 212 °F as the boiling point of water and 32 °F as the freezing point of water. The scale is divided into 180 units.

Body temperature
Disposable thermometers use chemicals that change colour in a temperature region either side of normal body temperature (which is about 36.5 °C. They are especially useful for rapid emergency use.

This is a thermometer designed to read maximum and minimum temperatures. As the temperature rises, colourless liquid in the bulb expands and pushes a thread of mercury around the tube. Small dumb-bell markers are moved around and are left behind at the maximum and minimum temperatures

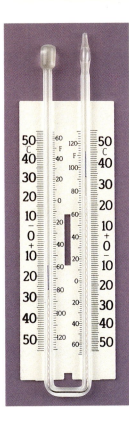

The Celsius scale
Temperature measured by the Celsius scale uses the boiling point of water as 100 °C and the freezing of ice as 0 °C. The scale is divided into 100 units as in the metric system.

Room temperature
Room temperatures are often controlled by a device set on the wall of the room or attached to each radiator. The 'controller' on the wall is a thermometer which can turn the central heating motor on and off; the 'controller' attached to a radiator is a thermometer which can close the water supply to the radiator when the room becomes sufficiently warm. The **valve** opens again if the room cools.

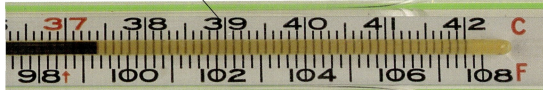

Temperature's colours
Temperature can change the behaviour of many chemicals. For example, one range of chemicals suddenly becomes clear when it reaches a certain temperature.

A strip thermometer measures temperature this way. A number of chemicals are painted on the strip which has a temperature scale printed on it. Each of the chemicals will become clear at a set temperature revealing the temperature printed underneath.

It is used where thermometers do not need great accuracy, such as in a refrigerator, or for domestic use.

A strip thermometer being used to measure temperature

Light and colour

Light is the energy that we receive from the Sun or any other shining object such as a light bulb.

Light comprises tiny particles and these can be measured as they fall on special sensitive materials.

Many cameras have light sensitive meters built in to them. When light shines on the sensitive material it makes a tiny electrical current and this is measured by a meter (see page 38).

Measure dyes
Many coloured materials are made of a mixture of dyes. You can find out what the different colours are in a water-based food dye or fountain pen ink by placing an upturned coffee filter paper in a saucer as shown on this page.

Make an ink or dye mark on the lower part of the paper and add clean water to the saucer as shown above.

As the water rises it draws up the different chemicals that make up the ink or dye. Each chemical has a different weight, and it gets drawn up the paper at different rate as you can see in the picture on the right.

(The measuring technique is called chromatography.)

Measure the light
You can use the **photoelectric cell** in a camera to find out how much light is being reflected from an object.

You need the kind of camera which has a light-meter built in or a separate light-meter.

Point the camera at the surface you want to measure and note the meter reading. You should make all readings in the same level of light, perhaps in the full sunlight. All measurements must be taken within a few minutes to make sure the strength of sunlight remains the same.

Electricity

Electricity is the flow of tiny particles called electrons along a wire, or some other conductor. Electrons can only flow when a loop or circuit is completed.

One easy way to measure that a circuit has been correctly wired is to include a light bulb in the circuit. When the current flows the bulb lights up.

However, the best way to find out what is happening inside a circuit is to make measurements with a meter.

This is a piece of a modern electronics board. It has no moving parts and the flow of electricity to and from the black boxes called integrated circuits can only be measured using a meter

A multimeter
This is an instrument for measuring the flow of electricity in a circuit.

The simple model here shows the principle that as a current flows from the battery through the wire a magnetic field is created. This, in turn, causes the magnetised needle to turn. The more electricity that flows in the wire, the more strongly the needle is deflected.

A multimeter measures the three main properties of electricity: voltage, current and resistance.

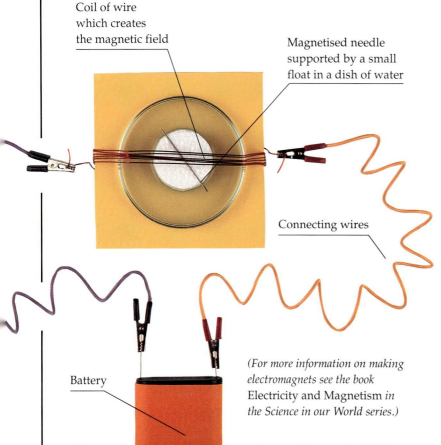

Coil of wire which creates the magnetic field

Magnetised needle supported by a small float in a dish of water

Connecting wires

Battery

(For more information on making electromagnets see the book Electricity and Magnetism *in the Science in our World series.)*

36

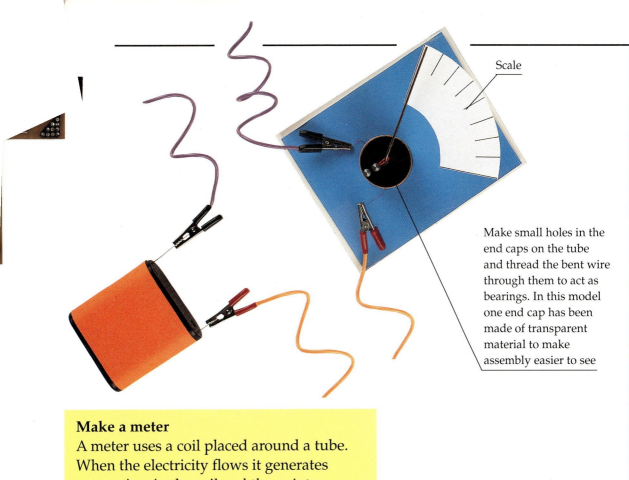

Scale

Make small holes in the end caps on the tube and thread the bent wire through them to act as bearings. In this model one end cap has been made of transparent material to make assembly easier to see

Make a meter

A meter uses a coil placed around a tube. When the electricity flows it generates magnetism in the coil and the pointer begins to turn.

You can make a simple meter using a coil of wire wound round a cardboard tube. The pointer is made from a bent piece of metal with a small rod-shaped magnet glued to it.

The coil is stuck on a baseboard.

Note: in a commercial multimeter the pointer is connected to a spring which returns the pointer to zero on the scale after each measurement

Bent wire for pointer

Baseboard

Coil wound round a cardboard tube

37

Using a meter

The most accurate way to measure electricity is by using a mulitmeter. Even a small pocket multimeter can be used to measure many of the properties of electricity.

Setting the meter
First decide what it is you are going to measure, then push the leads into the appropriate slots on the front of the meter and turn the knob until it points towards the type of measurement you want to make.

Take the leads from the meter and attach them to the object to be measured. The value can be read directly from the scale.

Caution
Household electricity is dangerous and can kill. Never try any experiments with household electricity or try to measure it.

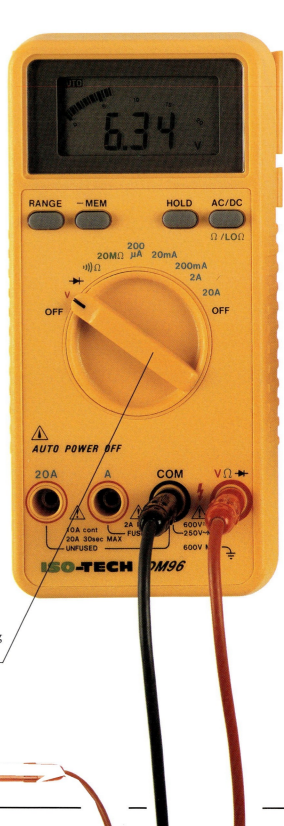

A meter set up to measure voltage. It is reading the voltage of a battery

Knob for changing the meter range

'Lie' detector?

You can measure the amount of resistance between two fingers of one hand by cutting a card to the shape of a hand and sticking strips of aluminium foil on to two of the fingers. Use clips to connect a meter to the aluminium strips, then set the meter to read resistance.

When someone places their hand on the card a tiny current will flow and the resistance will change. There are many things that affect the resistance including how much moisture is released by the sweat glands on the fingers. So if lying makes someone sweat more then it might show as a smaller resistance.

You can test the resistance of each person in a group – something you could not have told by looking at them!

Interpreting measurements

Making a measurement is not the same as deciding what that measurement really means. The 'lie detector' test is a very good example. It is, of course, not an accurate or reliable way to measure whether or not someone is telling the truth. So although a measurement will give you a value, it is still up to you to find the true sensible interpretation of that value.

39

Acidity

There is a bewildering number of chemicals to be found in our world. The food we eat is made up of chemicals, so is water, tea and coffee, and the bleach we use to clean the bathroom.

Two important types of chemicals are called **acids** and **alkalis**. Here are some ways to measure them.

Indicators

A substance that shows whether a chemical is an acid or an alkali is called an indicator. Some indicators come in liquid form.

Drops of indicator are put in a sample of the liquid to be tested. The indicator will change colour if the liquid is an acid, and it will turn a different colour if the liquid is an alkali.

Some indicators are made into paper strips by soaking in an indicator and allowing them to dry. They are used by dipping them in the liquid to be tested. Litmus paper is an example of a paper strip indicator.

Soil indicator

Farmers and gardeners need to know about the condition of their soils to get the best yields from the plants they want to grow.

Most crops do best in a soil that is between alkaline and very slightly acid. A special soil indicator is used to test for this.

The indicator is dropped into a glass tube containing a sample of soil and some **distilled water**. The tube is sealed and the contents shaken and allowed to settle. The indicator turns a green colour if the soil is alkali, yellow if slightly acid and bright red if strongly acid.

A soil that is too acid can be balanced by adding an alkali such as lime.

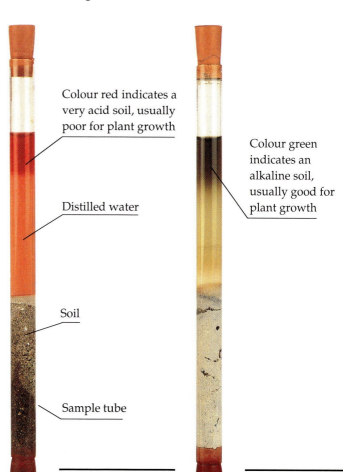

Colour red indicates a very acid soil, usually poor for plant growth

Distilled water

Soil

Sample tube

Colour green indicates an alkaline soil, usually good for plant growth

Warm water is poured over the chopped red cabbage

Cabbage leaf indicator

You can make an indicator with uncooked *red* cabbage leaves. You need to get some distilled water from the school laboratory or a chemist. *Tap water will not do.*

Boil the distilled water in a saucepan and add shredded red cabbage leaves. After a minute pour the leaves and water through a strainer and allow the liquid to stand until it is cool. It should be a pale blue colour.

You can use a small dropper to add cabbage indicator to a sample of the liquid to be tested. It will be easier to see the results if the sample is put in a small jar.

Alternatively you can soak some coffee filter paper discs in the cabbage water and then let the paper dry. Cut the paper into strips and use it like litmus paper.

Cabbage indicator turns green with an alkali and pink with an acid.

Try the indicator on a number of common household liquid foods and drinks. Also try other household items such as washing soda and vinegar.

The water is filtered off from the cabbage

Indicator	Strongly acid	Strongly alkaline

Bicarbonate of soda (alkali)

Vinegar (acid)

Pollution

Pollution is used to describe those unwanted substances in the environment that upset the natural pattern in our world.

There are many forms of pollution; some are solid, others liquids, and many are gases. The ideas on this page will help you to think about how you would tackle measuring such a problem. It is just one example of an application of measurement.

Samples of rain in tubes supplied with an acid rain testing kit

Acid rain

When gases from power stations and car exhausts get into the air they react with the tiny water droplets in clouds to make the water more acid than normal. When this acidic water falls as rain or snow it causes nutrients to be washed out of the soil and it dissolves other, harmful substances so they are taken up by plant roots or fish in streams.

To find out how much acid rain falls you will have to collect some rain in a jar and then either use the cabbage indicator described on page 41 or a special acid rain tester that is sold in shops. The special tester comes with a chart that allows you to make more accurate measurements of the degree of acidity.

A raingauge is easily made by cutting a soft drinks bottle in half and using the top as a funnel. The raingauge can then be placed in a flowerpot buried so that the top of the raingauge is level with the ground

Ground level

A filter paper made dirty by excessive levels of pollution in a city atmosphere

Water from a raingauge situated near a road

Dirty air and water

Dirt in the air may not be easy to see, but it is common in our environment.

To detect and measure dirt in the air put a coffee filter paper inside a kitchen funnel and stand it in a jar out in the open. This makes an improvised raingauge and it will give you an indication of how dirty the rainwater is.

To see how much dirt is clinging to leaves and other surfaces, wash the dirt off some leaves using washing up liquid. Collect the dirt from the water on a filter paper in a funnel. In a month repeat the experiment again and compare the amounts of dirt collected on the filter papers. This will show you how quickly the dirt builds up in your environment.

Try taking samples from several places around a town and compare the dirtiness of each place.

43

Samples

It is not always possible to measure all of something. Suppose we wanted to know how many daisy plants there were in a square kilometre of a meadow. It would take far too long to count every daisy in the meadow. Instead people choose several small parts of the meadow and find out how many plants there are in each.

Then they can scale up the results and in this way get a figure that will be quite close to the real number.

This method is called sampling. People are very careful how they choose their samples, because scaling up makes any error very big indeed.

A field of daisies

A quadrat

Quadrats

When studying plants, for example, many people use a frame called a quadrat (quadrat means square in Latin). You can make a quadrat from pieces of wood. A common size for a quadrat frame is for each side to measure half a metre. Quadrats are used by throwing the frame at random on to an area of ground and then counting and recording the chosen plants found within the frame. If a number of quadrat samples can be recorded in an area, the results can be averaged. This will make your final answer more accurate.

44

Sampling at random

You must not choose where to sample. Rather you must find a method of choosing a spot to measure by chance.

Sampling by chance, or at random, is rather like choosing a word from a page by being blindfolded and then putting your finger on the page.

One fun way of choosing where to sample is to throw dice. The diagram below represents a field that is to be sampled. A map has been obtained of the field and a set of lines drawn over it to make a grid. In this case, because we are going to use dice, the grid is made six squares by six squares.

Throw the dice, choosing the first one for left to right distance and the second one for up and down.

The quadrat can now be taken to the randomly chosen spot.

Dice

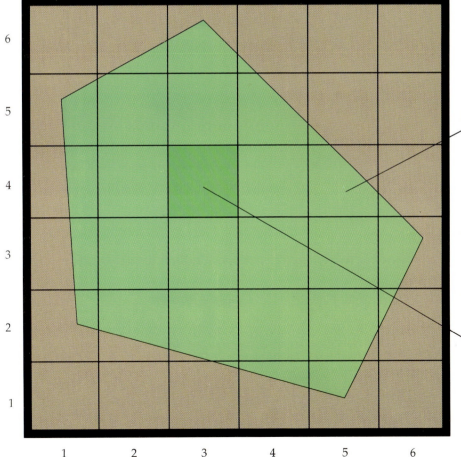

The field to be sampled

This square is chosen by throwing the dice. You can decide where to go in the square by dividing it up and throwing dice again

45

New words

acceleration
the increase in speed of an object. Acceleration is sometimes measured in the time it takes to reach a certain speed from a standing start. Deceleration is the opposite of acceleration, that is the rate of slowing down of an object

acid
any substance that dissolves in water and which corrodes anything it touches

alkali
any substance that dissolves in water and which is a derived from a mineral salt

arteries
the major blood vessels in the body

atmosphere
the shell of gases that surrounds the Earth. The atmosphere is divided into several layers, each with a distinctive property. The lowest layer is called the troposphere and it contains the clouds; above it is the stratosphere, a layer which contains protective ozone gas. The circulation of air in the troposphere gives rise to weather patterns

calibrate
to compare a measuring instrument with known standards so that it can be reliably used

capacity
the amount of volume that can be contained in a vessel when filled to the brim or to some other maximum mark made on its side

distilled water
water that has been boiled and then allowed to condense. Distilled water is free of the natural impurities that are found in tap or stream waters

fluid
a general name given to liquids and gases

friction
the natural stickiness between any two objects in the Universe. Friction occurs because all objects have a natural roughness, even though they may appear smooth to the naked eye. A liquid, called a lubricant, placed between two surfaces can help to keep them apart and reduce the value of friction

gravity
the force which acts throughout the Universe and which causes materials to come together. All the stars and the planets in the Universe are thought to have been pulled into shape by gravity. On Earth gravity pulls all objects towards the centre of the planet. A plumb line will therefore always point towards the Earth's centre

imperial system
an internally recognised system of measurements. The main units for measurement are the foot (ft) for length, the quart (qt) for volume, the pound (lb) for weight, the second (s) for time, the ampere (A) for electric current, and the degree Fahrenheit (F) for temperature

measuring cylinder
a tall glass or plastic vessel with straight sides and marked off in units of volume

metric system
an internationally recognised system of measurements based on the decimal system. The main units for measurement are the metre (m) for length, the litre (l) for volume, the kilogram (kg) for weight, the second (s) for time, the ampere (A) for electric current, and the degree Celsius (C) for temperature. The metric system is used throughout the world for scientific measurements even though many countries still maintain an Imperial system for everyday measurements

photoelectric cell
an electronic device made using a light-sensitive material. When light shines on the material it creates an electric current that can be used to do work such as showing the amount of light entering a camera

pivot
the place around which a bar or lever turns. It is usually made as a short shaft or pin and is commonly designed to move as freely as possible

rectangle
a four-sided figure in which all the angles between sides are right angles but where one pair of opposite sides have a different length from the other pair

revolution
one complete turn of a circle

spirit
a liquid which has been distilled usually by boiling. Spirits flow very easily and do not freeze as easily as water, which makes them suitable to use in levelling devices used in the open

stethoscope
an instrument consisting of a tube with a flat disc at one end, and a pair of earpieces at the together, connected by a flexible tube. The stethoscope allows sound waves made by pumping blood and other bodily activities to be easily heard by a doctor

valve
a flap or other means of blocking the flow of a gas or liquid

Index

acceleration   22, 23, 46
acid   40, 46
acid rain   42
alkali   40, 46
anemometer   29
area   10
arteries   27, 46
atmosphere   24, 46

balance   18
ball   17
barometer   24
blood pressure   27

cabbage leaf indicator   41
calibrate   9, 13, 19, 46
calliper   8
capacity   12, 46
Celsius   33
centre of gravity   30
chemicals   32, 34, 40
circle   16
circuit   36
circumference   17
cube   12
current   36

deceleration   23
diameter   17
dice   45
distance   6
distilled water   40, 46
dye   34

electricity   4, 34, 36
error   44

Fahrenheit   32
flow   28

fluid   24, 29, 46
friction   20, 46

gas   28
graph paper   11
gravity   30, 46
grid   45

height   12
horizontal   30

imperial system   5, 47
indicator   40

journey   9

kilogram   18

length   5, 6, 10
light   20, 21, 34
liquid   13, 26, 28
Litmus paper   40

magnetic field   36
manometer   26, 27
measuring cylinder
      15, 47
metric system   5, 47
multimeter   37

odometer   9

photoelectric cell   34, 47
pivot   19, 24, 47
plumb line   30
pollution   42
pressure   24, 26
profile   11

quadrat   44

radius   16
rain   42
rectangle   11, 47
resistance   39
revolution   9, 17, 47
road distances   9
ruler   6, 17

sampling   44
scale   18, 19, 21
second   4
soil   40, 42
speed   22
sphere   16
spirit level   31, 47
spring balance   18
squared paper   11
stethoscope   27, 47
streamers   28

tape   6
temperature   32
thermometer   32, 33
tracers   28

valve   33, 47
vane   28
velocity   22
vernier   9
vertical   30
volume   5, 12, 14, 15, 24

water   26, 28, 31
weather   24
weight   5, 18, 21
wheel   16
wind   28, 29

PATCHAM HIGH SCHOOL
LADIES MILE ROAD
BRIGHTON
EAST SUSSEX BN1 8PB